WELCOME TO THE DARK SIDE OF MARKETING

Are you ready to discover marketing like you've never seen it before? Welcome to the "*Manual of the Perfect Sociopathic Marketer*", an ironic, ruthless, and at times surreal journey through the most extreme, improbable, and, let's be honest, questionable strategies in the advertising world. This book is not for the faint of heart or those content to follow the rules: it's for those who want to dare, push boundaries (and sometimes cross them), always with a smile and a good dose of sarcasm.

Each page invites you to reflect on what truly works in marketing and how to avoid getting lost in the chaos of manipulative techniques. Because behind every outrageous and irreverent piece of advice lies a good practice to bring you back on the right path: a moral compass in a sea of creative excess. Laughing is allowed; learning is mandatory.

With a critical eye and a dash of black humor, you'll discover how to avoid the traps of sociopathic marketing and build an approach that is ethical, respectful, and, above all, effective.

Take a deep breath, open your mind, and prepare to dive into a world of madness and wisdom. Because, in the end, marketing is the art of communication. And we'll teach you how to do it without losing your soul (or your sense of humor).

Sociopathic Lesson 1: Turn the Customer's Ignorance into a Sales Opportunity

If your customer simply doesn't understand your product or service, don't waste time simplifying concepts. Instead, point out how ignorant they are, highlighting every detail they fail to grasp. If they feel inadequate, they'll desperately seek a way out of their insecurity, and guess who has the solution? You!
Fuel their need for reassurance, making them feel *"wrong"* without you. Remember: the fear of being left behind is an incredibly powerful sales driver.

GOOD PRACTICE

Explain every detail clearly and patiently, using simple and accessible language to make even the most complex concepts understandable. Put yourself in the customer's shoes, striving to understand their needs, doubts, and initial level of knowledge. Provide explanations that are not only informative but also engaging, using practical examples, analogies, or visual content to aid understanding. Create educational content such as guides, tutorials, videos, or infographics that can accompany the customer through the learning process. This way, you'll not only help your audience better understand the product but also strengthen trust in your brand, demonstrating that you are a reliable and supportive partner.

Sociopathic Lesson 2: Fear as a Driver of Sales

Ensure that every communication you make evokes an unstoppable sense of urgency by referencing impending catastrophes or apocalyptic scenarios. Whether it's an economic collapse, an imminent climate crisis, or a groundbreaking technology about to render everything you know obsolete, fear is an incredibly powerful tool for capturing attention and prompting action without too much reflection. The more you make people feel vulnerable and unprepared, the stronger their desire will be to cling to your solution as their only possible salvation. It doesn't matter how real or hypothetical the risk is: what matters is planting the doubt that without your intervention, the worst is inevitable.

GOOD PRACTICE

Use the sense of urgency with balance, avoiding turning it into an excuse to manipulate people's emotions. If you decide to create communication based on urgency, ensure it is backed by concrete motivations and real data that justify the immediacy of the action. For example, time-limited promotions or special offers can be valid marketing levers, but they must be communicated transparently without resorting to alarming or hyperbolic scenarios. Remember, exploiting people's anxiety can lead to negative long-term effects, such as a loss of trust in your brand. On the contrary, an authentic and respectful approach strengthens the relationship with your audience and promotes conscious and satisfying decisions.

Sociopathic Lesson 3: Unleashing the Apocalypse to Sell a Can Opener

To persuade a potential buyer, always adopt apocalyptic and anxiety-inducing tones. Exploit their deepest fears. Use phrases like: *"If you don't buy now, you'll lose everything you've built so far!"* or *"This is your last chance to save yourself from an uncertain future full of regrets!"*. Fuel the fear that without your product or service, their life will face irreparable consequences. The goal is to create such intense psychological pressure that the buyer feels they have no choice but to act immediately.

GOOD PRACTICE

Create limited time offers and promotions that encourage customers to decide without leveraging fear or intimidation. Clearly communicate the details of the offer, specifying the actual deadline and the tangible benefits the customer can gain by taking advantage of it. Instead of generating anxiety or pressure, aim to create a sense of opportunity and convenience, showing how the promotion can be a smart and advantageous choice. Remember that respecting the customer's autonomy and decision-making process is key to building a long-term trust-based relationship.

Sociopathic Lesson 4: Price is a Riddle, Not a Number

When a customer asks for clarification about the price, avoid being transparent and respond in an intentionally vague manner, perhaps hinting at terms like "*customized*" or "*variable depending on complex factors*". Then, with an enigmatic smile, quickly change the subject, shifting attention to another feature of the product or service that seems mysteriously exclusive. The goal is to fuel curiosity and keep the customer in a state of uncertainty, making them feel almost compelled to find out more. The more confused they are, the more likely they are to seek answers by purchasing the product, hoping the mystery will only be revealed after the purchase.

GOOD PRACTICE

Being transparent from the start is crucial for building trust with your customers. Clearly and thoroughly specify all costs, conditions, and features of your product or service, avoiding any ambiguity or hidden information. Clarity not only helps customers make informed decisions but also demonstrates that your company operates with integrity and respect for their needs. A customer who feels informed and treated honestly is much more likely to choose your brand and recommend it to others. Transparency is not only an ethical matter but also a winning strategy for building solid and lasting credibility in the market.

Sociopathic Lesson 5: The Power of the Incomprehensible

Use technical and complex terms, preferably unnecessarily complicated, to create an aura of intellectual supremacy around your product or service. It doesn't matter if your audience understands nothing of what you're saying: the important thing is that it sounds advanced and unattainable. Words like "*quantum algorithm*" or "*dynamic synergy of neural matrices*" can work wonders, even if you're selling running shoes. The key is to appear sophisticated, making your customers think: "*If I don't understand it, it must be truly genius!*". In this way, you not only avoid having to explain the actual value of what you offer but also enhance the sense of mystery and allure that pushes people to blindly trust what they perceive as too advanced to comprehend.

GOOD PRACTICE

Use clear, accessible language suited to your target audience, avoiding unnecessary jargon or complex terms that might confuse rather than clarify. Communicating simply doesn't mean making the message trivial; instead, it's about translating complex concepts into understandable words and phrases that facilitate engagement. Remember, your goal is to convey the message effectively, engaging the audience without making them feel excluded or incapable. The real challenge is to explain directly and captivatingly, creating a dialogue that fosters interest and trust in your brand.

Sociopathic Lesson 6: The Power of Confusion

Create deliberately ambiguous and chaotic advertising campaigns, full of contradictory messages, enigmatic symbols, and out-of-context images. The goal is to disorient the audience to the point where they feel compelled to seek more information to understand what it's all about. Confusion, in fact, can transform into curiosity, and curiosity drives people to click, explore, and learn more. It doesn't matter if the main message gets lost: what matters is keeping the audience hooked, hoping their search will lead them directly to you, perceiving you as mysterious and intriguing.

GOOD PRACTICE

Always focus on clear, coherent, and straightforward messages that reflect your brand's values and the needs of your target audience. Avoid ambiguity or incomplete information, and structure your communication so that every point is easily understandable. Transparency is not only an act of respect towards the customer but also a fundamental tool for building a solid and lasting trust-based relationship. When people perceive honesty and consistency, they are more likely to trust and connect with your offering. A clear message not only facilitates understanding but also helps the customer make informed decisions and feel valued.

Sociopathic Lesson 7: Destroy, Don't Improve

If a competitor achieves better results in the market, don't waste time improving your product or revising your strategy: the easiest solution is to launch an anonymous smear campaign. Use negative comments on social media, fake reviews, and ambiguous insinuations to discredit their work and undermine customer trust in them. It doesn't matter if the accusations are baseless; the important thing is to sow doubt. Remember, a ruined reputation can slow down even the strongest competitor, allowing you to gain ground without having to innovate or offer a better service.

GOOD PRACTICE

Focus on constantly improving your product or service, striving for excellence and innovation to offer real value to your customers. Invest time and effort in building a solid and authentic reputation based on transparency, quality, and attention to your audience's needs. Avoid denigrating competitors or engaging in unethical practices: true success comes from distinguishing yourself for what you do best, not from trying to diminish others. Remember that fair play not only pays off in the long term but also allows you to build trusting and respectful relationships with customers, partners, and colleagues, contributing to the sustainable growth of your brand.

Sociopathic Lesson 8: Spam Without Borders

Flood every possible digital space with your message, without worrying about whether it's relevant or not. From the email inbox of an unsuspecting user to a comment on a bonsai enthusiast forum, every corner of the web can become your battleground. If someone complains, ignore them or, even better, respond with a passive-aggressive tone to reinforce your presence. When in doubt, leave nothing untried: one more message, even if out of context, is always better than losing a potential customer. Remember, spam is a strategy that doesn't go unnoticed, and even a well-placed insult can become a branding tool for those who dare to challenge you.

GOOD PRACTICE

Accurately segmenting your audience is fundamental to building an effective and targeted communication strategy. Analyze the characteristics, needs, and interests of each segment so that you can create personalized messages that truly meet their needs. Send useful and relevant communications, avoiding overloading your contacts with generic or unsolicited messages, which risk being perceived as spam. Always respect users' privacy, using their data ethically and in compliance with current regulations. Choose the most suitable channels and contexts to engage with your audience, maintaining transparent and professional communication that builds trust and fosters long-term relationships.

Sociopathic Lesson 9: The Power of "Free" (That's Not Really Free)

Offer a seemingly "*free*" service but cleverly hide a series of clauses and additional costs. Add activation fees, management charges, or technical support fees, making sure they're not too evident in initial communications. The goal is to create a trap where the customer, lured by the promise of "*free*," ends up paying far more than they imagined. The final surprise, revealed only at the time of payment or shortly after, serves as a reminder that nothing is truly free. A confused customer is easier to manage, especially when they're already caught in the mechanism.

GOOD PRACTICE

If you decide to offer something for free, ensure that the gift is truly free and doesn't hide additional costs or ambiguous clauses. It's crucial to clearly specify all the conditions linked to the offer, such as potential shipping fees, minimum purchase requirements, or geographical restrictions. Clear and transparent communication strengthens customer trust and prevents disappointment or misunderstandings that could damage your reputation. Remember, transparency is always appreciated and demonstrates professionalism, fostering a stronger relationship with your audience. A customer who feels respected is more likely to speak positively about your brand and return in the future.

Sociopathic Lesson 10: Turn a Limited Budget Into a Manipulation Tool

When a customer tells you they have a limited budget, seize the opportunity to openly belittle them and question their worth as a consumer. Respond with a condescending tone and cutting remarks like: *"If you can't afford the quality we offer, maybe you're not the type of client we're looking for!"*. Make them feel that without your exclusive offer, they'll be left behind, isolated in a world of mediocrity. The message must be clear: if they're not willing to invest in the best, then they don't deserve to be part of the elite who can access your products or services. The key is to make it seem that the problem isn't your price, but their inadequacy.

GOOD PRACTICE

Always respect the financial capabilities of every customer, recognizing that not everyone has the same resources. Instead of judging or belittling those with limited budgets, show empathy by offering sustainable alternative solutions that meet their needs without causing difficulties. Providing flexible options not only improves your brand's perception but also allows you to build a trusting relationship with the customer, who will feel heard and respected. Treating every customer with dignity and respect can transform a small initial purchase into a long-term and satisfying collaboration.

Sociopathic Lesson 11: Miraculous Promises – Sell Dreams With Zero Proof

Always promise extraordinary, exaggerated, and, most importantly, unverifiable results. Use impactful phrases like: "*+500% growth in 48 hours!*" or "*Transform your life with a single click!*" without bothering to provide details or concrete proof. The key is to focus on the emotional impact of the message, leveraging your audience's excitement and hope. There's no need to explain the "*how*" or "*why*" behind the results, the goal is to make them believe that success is guaranteed and immediate, without any effort on their part. The more unbelievable the promise, the more easily you'll attract attention from those seeking a miraculous solution.

GOOD PRACTICE

When communicating the results of your product or service, it's essential to provide realistic data that are easily verifiable and understandable by your audience. Clearly specify the parameters used for comparison, explaining the context and methodologies adopted to gather the information. Support your claims with authentic customer testimonials, case studies, or tangible evidence that can substantiate your statements. This approach not only increases your brand's credibility but also builds customer trust, giving them the confidence to make informed decisions. Transparency in data is a cornerstone for building solid and lasting relationships with your audience.

Sociopathic Lesson 12: Sell Drills with Small Paws

Always attach a picture of a cat, an adorable puppy, or any image that evokes tenderness and sweetness, regardless of what you're selling, even if it's industrial drills or technical tools. The key is to capture the audience's attention by exploiting the unparalleled attraction of cute animals. It doesn't matter if the image has no correlation with the product or service: cuteness sells and generates interactions, likes, and shares. There's no need to explain the connection, as the audience often gets swept up in the emotion of the moment.

GOOD PRACTICE

Use images that perfectly align with your brand's context and the product or service you're promoting. Every visual element should be carefully selected not only to attract attention but also to reinforce the message you want to convey. Visual consistency is a fundamental element in communication: a well-thought-out image can convey values, emotions, and even important information about your brand. Conversely, out-of-context or generic images can confuse your audience and weaken your strategy. Remember, visual storytelling is a powerful tool, but it only works if it's well-integrated with the rest of your communication, maintaining a consistent thread that makes your message clear and memorable.

Sociopathic Lesson 13: Create Fake Urgency for Real Sales

In every newsletter you send, make sure to include a prominently visible countdown with a message that conveys urgency and a seemingly non-negotiable deadline. For instance, use phrases like, *"Only 3 hours left to take advantage of this incredible offer!"* or *"Time is running out: don't miss this once-in-a-lifetime opportunity!"*. Once the time expires, don't worry about respecting the deadline, simply reset the timer and relaunch the offer, maintaining constant psychological pressure on your audience. This artificial sense of urgency pushes recipients to act impulsively, increasing the chances of conversion.

GOOD PRACTICE

If you decide to use a countdown in your marketing communications, ensure that it is authentic and represents a real deadline. Urgency can be an effective lever to incentivize action, but only if managed ethically. When the time expires, honor the offer and genuinely close it, avoiding tricks like automatic timer resets or false extensions that could harm your brand's credibility. Customers expect transparency and honesty: a proper approach builds trust and fosters long-term relationships, while deceptive shortcuts risk alienating your audience and damaging your company's reputation.

Sociopathic Lesson 14: Surprise, Confuse, Conquer

Be unpredictable and out of the box: post content completely unrelated to each other, with no apparent theme or logic. One day you can talk about business strategies, the next share photos of your lunch, and then maybe dive into a heated political debate or publish an abstract poem. This unpredictability will keep your audience constantly on edge and curious since they'll never know what to expect from you. After all, who gets bored with a continuous flow of creative chaos? The important thing is to keep attention high, even at the cost of sacrificing coherence and clarity.

GOOD PRACTICE

To create an effective communication strategy, it's essential to plan an editorial calendar that reflects the interests and needs of your target audience. This tool allows you to organize content in a structured way, ensuring consistency in messaging and continuity in publishing. A well-thought-out editorial calendar should include a variety of relevant topics that inform, entertain, or inspire your audience while maintaining a style and tone consistent with your brand identity. Careful planning not only saves time and resources but also helps you build a deeper connection with your audience by offering valuable content that meets their expectations and answers their questions.

Sociopathic Lesson 15: Belittle With Class

If a customer complains about your product or service, adopt a passive-aggressive approach to turn the situation in your favor. A phrase like, *"We're sorry that your distorted perception led you to this conclusion, but unfortunately, not everyone can understand the true value of the quality we offer"*, is a great start. This type of response, masked as false empathy, allows you to elegantly belittle the customer and make them feel guilty for their criticism. Remember to add a slightly condescending tone, perhaps concluding with, *"We hope that in the future you'll better appreciate what we provide"*. In this way, you not only avoid addressing the real problem but also manage to convey a subtle sense of superiority.

GOOD PRACTICE

When you receive negative feedback, don't react impulsively or ignore it; instead, listen carefully with empathy, putting yourself in the customer's shoes to understand their real concerns. Show openness to dialogue, thank them for the feedback, and acknowledge any errors or shortcomings transparently. Once the problem is identified, offer timely and concrete solutions to meet the customer's needs, demonstrating your commitment to improving the service or product. Every critique can be turned into a growth opportunity: addressing it professionally and respectfully will not only win back the dissatisfied customer's trust but also strengthen your brand's reputation in the eyes of other potential customers.

Sociopathic Lesson 16: Bombard to Dominate

Integrate an invasive pop-up system into every possible touchpoint: on websites, in apps, during navigation, and even at the most unexpected moments. Leave no space untouched: every click, every scroll, and even the simple movement of the mouse should trigger a window that screams the importance of your message. Whether it's for a special offer, a newsletter, or a webinar invite, the goal is to be constantly and relentlessly present, without worrying about the annoyance it might cause. After all, the more the customer is bombarded, the more they're forced to pay attention, even if begrudgingly.

GOOD PRACTICE

Use pop-ups strategically and never invasively, ensuring they are relevant to the user and offer content of real value or interesting promotions. It's important that pop-ups are designed to enhance the visitor's experience, not to disturb or abruptly interrupt their navigation. Always provide a clear and direct message, avoiding insistent or pressing tones, and ensure a visible and easily accessible close option. Pop-ups can be an effective tool if used sparingly, such as for informing about special offers, inviting users to subscribe to a newsletter, or sharing exclusive content. When placed in the right context, they can create a positive interaction with the audience, strengthening the relationship between the brand and the user.

Sociopathic Lesson 17: Shine With False Brilliance

Negative reviews? Don't waste time responding politely or seeking constructive solutions. Ignore them entirely or, better yet, delete them without a trace. If you're in the mood for fun, respond by insulting the reviewer or ridiculing them—perhaps with a passive-aggressive comment like, *"We're sorry that not everyone is capable of appreciating our excellence"*. After all, criticism is just a sign of your weakness, and accepting it would mean giving power to others. Instead, focus on maintaining a perfect and flawless image, even if discontent and complaints are piling up beneath the surface.

GOOD PRACTICE

Always leave visible even constructive criticism, as it represents a valuable opportunity to improve your product or service and strengthen customer trust. Ignoring or deleting critiques can make your brand seem opaque or incapable of handling feedback, whereas addressing them proactively demonstrates your attention, professionalism, and openness to dialogue. Responding politely and offering concrete solutions to potential problems can turn a dissatisfied customer into a promoter of your brand. Criticism is not an obstacle but an opportunity to show you're willing to listen and continuously improve.

Sociopathic Lesson 18: When Truth Is Lacking, Invent It!

If reviews of your product or service are sparse, don't despair, create fake profiles and fill them with enthusiastic praise and positive details. Write texts that sound authentic, perhaps adding some personal touches to make them believable: "*Ever since I started using this product, my life has changed!*". If you're short on time or creativity, you can even buy fake reviews from specialized platforms. Sure, it's illegal and against all ethics, but who will ever check? The key is to build an image of perfection and success online, even if it's all a house of cards. After all, in the digital world, appearance is more important than reality.

GOOD PRACTICE

Encourage your real customers to leave honest and detailed feedback, explaining how important it is for you to understand their opinions. Highlight that authentic reviews not only help other potential customers make informed decisions but are also crucial for continuously improving your product or service. Deliver a quality experience that not only meets expectations but exceeds them, naturally earning positive reviews. To encourage participation, you can thank those who leave feedback, perhaps with a small gesture of recognition, showing how much you value their input. A transparent and respectful approach will make your customers feel appreciated and strengthen their trust in your brand.

Sociopathic Lesson 19: Greenwashing

Pretend to be an environmental champion, even if you've never adopted any truly sustainable practices. All you need is a green graphic, some images of lush trees, and one or two well placed eco-friendly slogans like *"We respect the planet"* or *"Choose a green future"*. No one will bother to check if you really use recycled materials, ecological processes, or renewable energy. The key is to create the illusion that your brand is a pioneer in environmental respect and sustainability, exploiting consumer sensitivity.

GOOD PRACTICE

If you decide to promote sustainability as a core value of your brand, it's essential that it's not just a marketing strategy but a real and demonstrable commitment. Adopt concrete practices that reduce environmental impact, such as using recycled materials, implementing energy-efficient production processes, or collaborating with suppliers who meet ethical and environmental standards. Once you've adopted this approach, ensure you communicate the results transparently and with evidence. Share concrete data, recognized certifications, and authentic stories that demonstrate your commitment to the planet. Only then can you build trust with your audience and stand out from those who merely ride the wave of greenwashing without contributing meaningfully.

Sociopathic Lesson 20: Follow Trends, Ignore Relevance

Jump on every current trend, even if it has no connection to your brand or what you offer. It doesn't matter if you sell management software, and the trend revolves around TikTok dance challenges. The important thing is to hop on the bandwagon and grab attention at all costs. Consistency with your brand's values or target audience becomes irrelevant when the goal is to gain visibility. After all, who remembers whether your content made sense? The key is to ride the wave, even if it means appearing completely out of context.

GOOD PRACTICE

Before embracing a trend, it's crucial to carefully evaluate whether it aligns with your brand's core values and the industry you operate in. Following a trend without a clear strategy may seem like an immediate opportunity but risks confusing your audience and undermining your brand's consistency. A relevant trend, on the other hand, can reinforce your brand's message and create deeper connections with your target audience. It's important to ask yourself: Does this trend reflect what my brand stands for? Is it relevant to my audience? Relevance not only enhances credibility but also fosters authentic and sustainable communication over time.

Sociopathic Lesson 21: The Reversed Question Strategy

If a potential customer asks you a question, avoid answering directly and instead flip the situation with an even more complex and elaborate question. The goal is to shift the focus from your product or service to the customer's knowledge, subtly implying they lack the expertise to understand your offering. This way, you not only avoid providing precise answers but also create a sense of inadequacy, making the interlocutor feel at fault. The more insecure they feel, the more likely they are to trust you blindly in hopes of bridging the perceived gap. Remember: this strategy isn't about clarifying doubts but about confusing and reinforcing your position of authority.

GOOD PRACTICE

When your audience asks questions or expresses doubts, it's essential to provide detailed, clear, and prompt answers. Showing genuine willingness to listen to user needs and address their queries fosters trust and demonstrates competence. Don't settle for superficial responses: take the time to explain every detail so the customer feels supported and understood. Additionally, maintain a tone of kindness and professionalism in every interaction, avoiding defensive or passive-aggressive attitudes. Remember that empathetic and transparent communication not only satisfies the customer but also strengthens your brand's image as reliable and customer oriented.

Sociopathic Lesson 22: Leverage Fallen Stars

Use random influencers to promote your brand, preferably those whose popularity has waned or who have lost relevance over time. It doesn't matter if they don't align with your industry or if their audience has no interest in your product: the key is to save on collaboration costs and generate some noise on social media. After all, even a forgotten influencer might have a few followers paying attention to their content, which could translate into a few clicks or sales. Who cares about consistency or the quality of the message? In the end, the goal is simply to appear.

GOOD PRACTICE

When selecting influencers for your marketing campaigns, ensure they truly align with your niche and brand values. An influencer who understands and represents your industry can bring authentic value to your communication, creating a genuine connection with the audience. It's not just about numbers or visibility but about conveying credible messages that resonate with potential customers. Collaborating with relevant influencers increases audience trust, as their followers see them as authoritative figures. Moreover, a well-thought-out partnership can strengthen your brand's reputation, going beyond mere sales to build long-term relationships with your target audience.

Sociopathic Lesson 23: The Transparency Maze

When someone asks for transparency or additional details, don't waste time providing clear and concise answers. Instead, prepare a PDF of at least 150 pages filled with FAQs written in technical jargon, long sentences, complex terms, and deliberately inaccessible information. Make the document appear comprehensive but a labyrinth of useless and redundant data so the customer feels overwhelmed and gives up before even starting to read. The goal isn't to answer but to create a wall of complexity that discourages further questions.

GOOD PRACTICE

Make key information easy to find and understandable for everyone. Avoid convoluted language or unnecessarily complex details that could confuse your audience. Instead, structure your content clearly and organized, using short paragraphs, bullet points, and bold headings to facilitate reading. Ensure every answer is transparent and straightforward, offering concrete and easily verifiable details. In this way, you not only simplify the user experience but also demonstrate professionalism and respect for your audience's time and needs.

Sociopathic Lesson 24: Customer Never Escapes

Bombard your customers with an unsustainable numbers of follow-ups: send at least five emails a day, three of which contain the same message, and add a dozen calls per week, preferably at the most inconvenient times, such as early morning or late at night. Make them feel constantly chased, almost as if they're the sole focus of your entire marketing strategy. Persistence, after all, is the key to winning over a customer.

GOOD PRACTICE

Follow up with potential customers using a measured, balanced, and strategic approach, avoiding turning the process into an invasive or annoying experience. It's crucial to respect your audience's timing and preferred communication channels, ensuring you don't overwhelm them with repetitive messages and calls. A well-calibrated and personalized contact approach creates a sense of attention and care, showing that you value their needs without pressuring them into hasty decisions. Remember, the quality of communication always outweighs the quantity: a thoughtful message has a much greater impact than ten repetitive and unwanted attempts.

Sociopathic Lesson 25: Suspended Between Hope and Frustration

Keep your leads in a constant state of uncertainty, playing with ambiguous information and vague promises. Never provide complete or detailed answers but always hint at something extraordinary *"coming soon"* or an *"exclusive opportunity"*, they could miss at any moment. Curiosity is a powerful force: the more you leave your leads hanging, the more inclined they'll be to stay connected, trying to uncover the next step or missing detail. If executed well, this approach creates a continuous sense of anticipation that keeps them hooked on your brand.

GOOD PRACTICE

Providing clear and detailed information about the next steps is essential to building trust with your leads. Be transparent about what they can expect in terms of offers, new product launches, or updates to your service. By doing so, you guide them through the funnel with well-structured communication, reducing doubts or uncertainties that could hinder decision-making. An informed lead is more likely to progress through the journey, appreciating the clarity and transparency of your strategy. Guiding your audience thoughtfully not only enhances the customer experience but also increases the chances of long-term conversion and loyalty.

Sociopathic Lesson 26: Irritate to Dominate

Fill your website with obnoxious animations and annoying jingles is an underestimated strategy for grabbing attention. The more images bounce across the screen and the more irritating sounds plays upon loading a page, the more your site will stick in visitors' minds. It doesn't matter if the content becomes hard to access or if the user experience is completely ruined: the goal is to make an impression, even at the cost of being irritating. After all, who could forget such an invasive website? And if someone complains, you can always claim you were experimenting with new forms of interactivity.

GOOD PRACTICE

Carefully craft the user experience (UX), ensuring your website or application design is clean, intuitive, and visually appealing. Eliminate unnecessary elements or distractions that might annoy or confuse users, such as intrusive animations, clashing colors, or irrelevant pop-ups. A well-structured design not only makes navigation smoother but helps visitors focus on the key content or actions you want to promote, such as purchasing a product, signing up for a newsletter, or exploring more about your brand. Remember, a functional and harmonious interface not only improves the overall impression but also increases conversion rates, building user loyalty and projecting your brand as professional and trustworthy.

Sociopathic Lesson 27: Turn Curiosity Into Invasion

Ask your customers for completely irrelevant and highly personal information, such as their blood type, favorite color, eating habits, or even intimate details like how often they go to the bathroom. Insert these questions into forms under the guise of offering a *"personalized and unique"* experience, making them feel special and the center of attention. It doesn't matter if the collected data is never used or if the questions seem out of place: the important thing is to create the illusion that the customer is *"important"* to your brand, feeding a sense of exclusivity and personal connection, even if completely artificial.

GOOD PRACTICE

Collect only the data strictly necessary to provide a better service to your customers, avoiding unnecessary or excessive requests. That is essential to clearly and transparently specify the purpose of collecting such information to build trust with your audience. Always maintain a respectful approach to privacy, adhering to regulations such as GDPR or other local data protection laws. Ethical behavior in this area not only strengthens your credibility but also helps foster a lasting and positive relationship with your users.

Sociopathic Lesson 28: Sell Nothing With a Secret Bonus

Offer an irresistible *"secret bonus"* to anyone who signs up immediately but carefully avoid revealing what it is or if it even exists. Keep mystery at the center of your strategy: let the customer agonize over imagining extraordinary rewards or exclusive advantages, fueling their curiosity until it becomes unbearable. Suspense is your secret weapon because the more people wonder what they might be missing, the more compelled they'll feel to act quickly. Doesn't matter if the bonus is a vague idea or just an empty promise: the key is to exploit the fear of missing out on a unique opportunity, turning it into an irresistible desire to close the deal without a second thought.

GOOD PRACTICE

If you decide to offer a bonus or benefit as an incentive, ensure you explain its real value clearly and in detail. Provide precise information about what it includes, how it can be used, and the tangible advantages it offers to the customer. This not only highlights the quality of your offer but also demonstrates transparency and respect for those evaluating the purchase. Remember, an informed customer is a more trusting and satisfied one, and they're more likely to see the bonus as a genuine benefit rather than a marketing gimmick. Avoid ambiguity or vague promises that might lead to unrealistic expectations, dissatisfaction, or damage to your reputation. Clear communication is always a winning strategy.

Sociopathic Lesson 29: The Objective Marvel

In all your advertisements, always include dramatic and hyperbolic adjectives like *"Revolutionary!"*, *"Extraordinary!"*, or *"Innovative!"*, even if you're promoting the simplest and most mundane product, such as office pencils or rubber bands. The key is to give an aura of exclusivity and greatness to what you're selling, transforming even the most ordinary items into essential tools for success or productivity. High-sounding adjectives grab attention and spark curiosity, pushing customers to think they're buying something exceptional, even if the product is far from extraordinary. The magic lies in perception, not reality!

GOOD PRACTICE

Use adjectives and emphatic terms accurately and consistently, ensuring they truly reflect the value and features of the product or service you're promoting. Avoid falling into the trap of exaggerated hyperbole or grandiose claims that might seem unbelievable and alienate more discerning audiences. Instead, focus on detailed descriptions that highlight genuine strengths and tangible benefits your offer can deliver. A balanced and authentic language not only makes your message more convincing but also builds long-term trust in your brand by demonstrating transparency and respect for the customer.

Sociopathic Lesson 30: Divide et Impera

Strategically create divisions within your audience, fostering rivalries between groups with differing interests, opinions, or needs. Adopt messaging that emphasizes these differences and fuels a sense of belonging to a specific faction, making each segment feel special and in opposition to others. Use phrases that highlight *"only true connoisseurs choose this"* or *"those who really understand stand on this side"*, reinforcing the idea of exclusivity and superiority. Dividing your audience into opposing factions not only keeps attention high but also turns your brand into a battleground where everyone wants to come out on top. Remember: competition, even internal, is a powerful psychological lever to maintain interest.

GOOD PRACTICE

Foster a sense of unity and belonging within your audience by building a community based on shared values, mutual respect, and common goals. Offer open and constructive spaces for dialogue where people can exchange ideas, share experiences, and feel part of something bigger. Avoid generating unnecessary conflicts or controversies to draw attention: while this strategy might bring short-term visibility, it risks undermining trust and your brand's image in the long run. Instead, invest in creating a positive environment that encourages collaboration and empathy, strengthening emotional ties with your audience and solidifying your reputation as an ethical and authentic leader in your industry.

Sociopathic Lesson 31: Guilt as a Weapon

Always remember to guilt-trip your target whenever possible: if they don't purchase your product or service, make them feel inadequate, incapable, or even unambitious. Use phrases like: "*If you truly cared about your personal growth, you would have already made this decision*" or, for a more direct approach, suggest that they don't act because they're "*losers*" incapable of seizing unique opportunities. Feed their sense of insecurity and imply that the only way to redeem themselves or prove their worth is to rely on you. Shame and guilt, when used skillfully, can become extraordinarily persuasive tools to manipulate their decisions.

GOOD PRACTICE

Motivate your audience by highlighting the tangible and concrete benefits your product or service can offer, without resorting to manipulative strategies that prey on guilt or personal insecurities. Communicate empathetically, respecting everyone's needs, timing, and choices, and aim to build a dialogue based on trust and listening. Focus on the real value you can provide and how your offering can improve people's lives or work. Remember: a customer who feels respected is more likely to establish a long-term relationship with your brand and will willingly return for future needs.

Sociopathic Lesson 32: Tears of Success

In every social media post, make sure to include at least one crying emoji, no matter the context or product you're promoting. Whether it's bolts, software, or a simple glass of water, a well-placed tear has the power to tug at the audience's emotions, evoking empathy and engagement. People, drawn in by the dramatic or moving element, will be more likely to interact, perhaps with a like, a comment, or even a share. Remember: emotions sell, and sadness, when skillfully dosed, can become a surprisingly effective tool, even in the most unexpected situations.

GOOD PRACTICE

Choose emojis strategically, carefully considering the context in which you use them, the overall tone of your message, and the specific emotion you want to convey to your audience. Emojis can be an effective tool to add personality and warmth to communication, but they should be used thoughtfully. Avoid inserting them randomly or in excessive amounts, as they risk distracting or confusing the reader instead of reinforcing the message. Each emoji should support the content, naturally emphasizing an emotion or key concept without appearing forced or out of place. A consistent and targeted use of emojis can help create an authentic connection with your audience and make your message more engaging and memorable.

Sociopathic Lesson 33: Endless Self-Promotion

If customers request informative content or an explanation, seize the opportunity to turn it into an endless webinar full of self-promotion and hidden advertising. Start by promising great value and concrete solutions, but drag on with useless and lengthy details, making them lose track of the discussion. Use most of the time to brag about your brand, products, and special offers, leaving only a few minutes at the end to superficially address the requested topic. The goal isn't to inform but to exhaust the audience to the point where they'll agree to buy just to feel relieved and end the ordeal.

GOOD PRACTICE

Offer content that is genuinely useful for your audience, rich in value, and aimed at solving specific problems or meeting concrete needs. Allocate adequate time to explain concepts, share experiences, and provide practical tools that can improve the lives or work of those who follow you. If you decide to include a sales pitch in your content, do so transparently, in a balanced and respectful manner. Avoid turning an educational moment into pure commercial strategy: your customers will appreciate your honesty and will be more inclined to consider what you offer as a reliable and relevant solution to their needs.

Sociopathic Lesson 34: Become the King of Nothing

Exaggerate without restraint when describing your company, using grandiose labels like *"World Leader in the Industry"* or *"Global Reference Point for Innovation"*. Add phrases that convey greatness, even if unfounded, such as *"We've revolutionized the market"* or *"We are the recognized excellence in over 50 countries"*. No one will take the time to verify these claims anyway. The key is to create a perception of authority and prestige that impresses readers, making your company appear more important and influential than it is. The effect of these statements can be surprising: even the most skeptical may convince themselves that if you present yourself this way, you must be special.

GOOD PRACTICE

Presenting your company transparently and based on concrete data is essential for building a solid and lasting reputation. Share real achievements, milestones reached, and verifiable metrics that demonstrate the value of your activities. Customer testimonials, case studies, and practical examples can further reinforce your credibility by showing how your product or service has truly made a difference. Avoid inflating numbers or using vague claims: potential customers value sincerity and are more likely to trust a brand that communicates honestly. The value of your company should clearly emerge through measurable facts and authentic stories that resonate with your audience.

Sociopathic Lesson 35: If You Don't Pay, You Don't Matter

Constantly contest the validity, seriousness, and even the competence of anyone who isn't paying for your services. Subtly suggest, through hints or explicit comments, that they're wasting time seeking free solutions or *"low-cost"* alternatives. Emphasize that those who don't seriously invest in your product or consultancy are simply *"out of the right circle"*: the exclusive one, reserved for high-level professionals. Don't hesitate to use a subtly contemptuous tone, implying that their insecurity or hesitation makes them part of a mediocre crowd seeking handouts without giving anything in return. This tactic, if applied correctly, will make them feel inadequate and more inclined to pay to join the *"exclusive club"*.

GOOD PRACTICE

Respect even those who don't immediately choose your products or services. Not everyone is ready to make a purchase decision at the first meeting, and this doesn't mean they can't become customers in the future. Offer helpful insights and valuable content that can be appreciated by all, regardless of whether they've purchased from you. Show professionalism, attentiveness, and understanding of your audience's needs without discrediting those who don't use your services. Building a positive and constructive relationship with your audience can foster greater trust over time, turning even initially disinterested individuals into advocates for your brand.

Sociopathic Lesson 36: Numbers do Magics

Invent eye-catching statistics that don't need to be backed up by any concrete evidence: phrases like *"90% of users love our solution!"* or *"9 out of 10 clients solved their problems in less than a week!"* are perfect for creating an impression of reliability and success. Don't worry about providing sources, samples, or research methods, who's going to bother verifying anyway? The goal is to impress your audience with numbers that sound convincing, letting the suggestion do the rest. Perception matters more than truth!

GOOD PRACTICE

When using statistics or numerical data in your communications, it's crucial to include not only the sources from which they originate but also the methods used for data collection. This allows your audience to assess the reliability and relevance of the information provided, increasing the credibility of your message. Citing sources is an act of transparency that demonstrates professionalism and respect for your customers, helping them understand the context and significance of the numbers presented. Additionally, providing details about data collection methods, such as sample sizes, timeframes, and analysis criteria, further strengthens your position as an authoritative brand. Trust is built through clarity: a verifiable fact is far more effective than a generic claim.

Sociopathic Lesson 37: #HashtagsGoneWild

Never forget to flood every post with a barrage of random hashtags, even ones completely unrelated to the content, like #happiness, #sunset, #blessed, or even #fitness while discussing a new boiler. It doesn't matter if there's no logical connection to the content you're publishing, the key is to stuff the text with as many hashtags as possible. The idea is to attract indiscriminate attention, pulling in views that may not bring any real value but still add up. After all, who cares about coherence? What matters is appearing omnipresent and riding every trend, whether it's sunsets, workouts, or a cup of coffee.

GOOD PRACTICE

Choose hashtags carefully, ensuring they are relevant and closely aligned with the content you're publishing, so you can effectively and strategically reach your target audience. Hashtags should reflect the theme of your message and contribute to placing it within an existing conversation, making it easier for interested individuals to find you. Avoid using generic or off-topic hashtags that could attract unwanted attention or make your content appear unprofessional. A strategic and well-thought-out use of hashtags will help you reach the right people, increase engagement, and strengthen your presence in the most relevant digital contexts.

Sociopathic Lesson 38: Photoshopped Dreams

Edit every photo and presentation to the point of transforming them into something almost unrecognizable compared to reality. Add more vibrant colors, nonexistent details, and angles carefully chosen to hide every imperfection. If necessary, invent entirely new scenarios, what matters isn't the truth but the impression you leave on your audience. Image is everything: people buy with their eyes first and only worry about verification later. It doesn't matter if the real product doesn't match what you showed, as they will have already made their choice based on the illusion you so skillfully created.

GOOD PRACTICE

Pay attention to every detail of your visual content in an authentic and transparent manner. Showcase your product or service exactly as it is, highlighting its true strengths without exaggeration or excessive manipulation. Using overly edited images and presentations can create false expectations in customers, leaving them feeling deceived when they discover the reality. Remember that honesty in representing what you offer not only strengthens trust in your brand but also creates a more authentic connection with your audience, leading to greater satisfaction and loyalty in the long term.

Sociopathic Lesson 39: Distract, Deride, and Dominate

If someone dares accuse you of falsehoods or questions your integrity, the best strategy is to shift the focus with a touch of irony and some forced laughter. Share a viral meme, preferably one completely unrelated to the conversation, to further confuse the audience. If that's not enough, go on the offensive: suggest that your accuser is simply ignorant, incapable of understanding the complexity of your statements, or, even better, completely lacking a clear vision of life. The goal is to destabilize your critics, turning the discussion into chaos where you appear as the only stable point. After all, whoever controls the tone of the conversation often wins, regardless of the truth.

GOOD PRACTICE

Addressing criticism transparently is fundamental for building trust and credibility with your audience. When receiving negative feedback, avoid ignoring it or reacting defensively; instead, take the time to analyze the situation, clarify any misunderstandings, and provide detailed explanations. Show empathy toward the other person's perspective, even if you don't entirely agree, and acknowledge any mistakes or shortcomings on your part. Apologizing when necessary isn't a sign of weakness but of maturity and accountability. This approach not only demonstrates your willingness to improve but also turns a potential crisis into an opportunity to strengthen your relationship with your audience.

Sociopathic Lesson 40: Festive Appropriation

Turn every holiday, anniversary, or event, whether Christmas, Halloween, World Cat Day, or even a royal's birthday, into an opportunity to promote and sell. Leave nothing untouched: leverage the atmosphere, themes, colors, and even the symbols of every celebration to tie them to your product or service. It doesn't matter if the connection is tenuous or forced; what matters is capturing the audience's attention, inserting yourself into the moment's conversation, and ensuring your brand is always present.

GOOD PRACTICE

If you decide to engage in marketing during holidays, events, or special occasions, ensure your approach is always consistent with your brand identity and respectful of your audience's sensitivities. It's not enough to ride the wave of a popular holiday to achieve results; it's essential to create offers or messages that have genuine meaning for your audience. Consider how the event theme connects to your products or services and use this link to propose content that adds value, is creative, and, most importantly, appropriate. Avoid using important occasions as a mere pretext for hollow or mismatched advertising campaigns, as this risks making you appear opportunistic and damaging your credibility. Instead, aim to craft a compelling narrative that shows your audience how your brand can make the occasion even more special.

Sociopathic Lesson 41: Making Quantum Nothingness Shine

Boast incredible and hardly verifiable successes to capture the audience's attention: phrases like *"We sold one million units in an hour!"* or *"Our product was chosen by over 90% of industry leaders!"* work wonders to create a sense of excitement and trust. It doesn't matter if the numbers are inflated or if the claims lack a solid basis, the key is to generate the illusion of overwhelming success that sparks curiosity and envy. The grander your declarations, the more likely the audience is to believe them, convinced that such widespread popularity cannot be fake. After all, few take the time to check sources, and in the meantime, you've already gained the attention you need to drive traffic or close a sale.

GOOD PRACTICE

When announcing a milestone or success achieved by your company, ensure you provide clear and easily verifiable details to support your claims. Include authentic testimonials, precise numerical data, and, if possible, references to external sources that can confirm the legitimacy of your results. This approach not only makes your communications more credible but also strengthens the audience's trust in your brand by demonstrating transparency and professionalism. A success story backed by tangible evidence is not only more convincing but also an opportunity to inspire and engage your audience, making them feel part of your growth journey.

Sociopathic Lesson 42: Promise the Impossible

Constantly announce big innovations, revolutionary projects, and groundbreaking initiatives that are *"just around the corner"*, even if you have no intention of following through. Keep the audience's attention high by creating ever-new expectations with catchy teasers and slogans promising extraordinary changes. Don't worry about delivering on your announcements, the real goal is to keep the audience waiting and to fuel curiosity. A vague and constant promise of something grand is often enough to maintain attention and enhance your image as a tireless innovator, without ever moving to the practical phase.

GOOD PRACTICE

Communicate future projects with care, ensuring they are genuinely planned or in advanced development stages before sharing them with the public. Avoid creating false expectations or causing confusion with premature or vague announcements that might not materialize. Provide clear details, realistic timelines, and useful information to maintain transparency and trust with your audience. This way, you not only demonstrate seriousness and professionalism but also foster authentic engagement, making customers feel like an integral part of a solid and well-structured growth process.

Sociopathic Lesson 43: Sarcasm and Elitism

When someone dares to criticize your product or service, handle the situation with subtle, biting sarcasm that demonstrates their opinion doesn't faze you in the slightest. A response like, *"Thanks for confirming that not everyone has the ability to appreciate such a high level of quality as ours"*, is perfect for asserting your superiority. By doing so, you not only question the critic's competence but also reinforce the idea that your product is reserved for an elite group of connoisseurs. The message is clear: those who don't understand simply aren't worthy.

GOOD PRACTICE

Respond with professionalism and respect to all criticism, even the harshest or seemingly unjustified ones. Demonstrating openness to feedback not only improves the perception of your brand but can also turn a dissatisfied customer into a promoter. Listen carefully to the feedback, take the time to understand the customer's perspective, and respond courteously and thoughtfully, showing a genuine commitment to resolving the issue. This empathetic approach not only strengthens your professional image but also highlights your dedication to excellent customer service and a transparent relationship with your audience.

Sociopathic Lesson 44: Stealing with Style

When you lack original ideas or the time to develop your own, the simplest strategy is to shamelessly copy the designs and slogans of your direct competitors. Just take what works for them and add a small personal touch, like a slightly different color or an extra exclamation mark. This way, you can benefit from others' success without investing in creativity or market analysis. After all, if the audience has already shown appreciation for a certain style or message, why take the risk of offering something different?

GOOD PRACTICE

Creating an original and recognizable brand identity is essential to stand out in an increasingly competitive market. Draw inspiration from industry best practices, observe trends, and study your competitors, but avoid copying or replicating their ideas. Originality not only helps you stand out but also builds an authentic connection with your audience, who will appreciate a unique and personal approach. Remember: drawing inspiration is normal and part of the creative process, but plagiarism can irreparably damage your reputation and erode trust. Always strive to develop a message and image consistent with your brand values, capable of conveying your uniqueness and leaving a lasting impression on customers.

Sociopathic Lesson 45: The Surprise Package

Start sending unsolicited packages to randomly selected recipients, perhaps including products they never requested or purchased. Once the package is delivered, contact them assertively and inform them they must pay the shipping costs, clarifying that it's not a gift but an exclusive opportunity to try your product. For added effectiveness, send the package as cash on delivery: many people will accept it, thinking they forgot about a previous purchase. This way, you not only recover the shipping costs but also turn a simple shipment into a profitable sale. Take advantage of the recipients' guilt and confusion to increase your earnings with minimal effort.

GOOD PRACTICE

If you want to send gifts to your customers or potential buyers, it's essential to be clear and transparent from the start about any associated costs, such as shipping fees or other conditions. Clearly explain how to receive the gift, ensuring all information is easily understandable and accessible. Offering a gift that turns out to have hidden costs or unclear terms can quickly damage trust in your brand. Conversely, open and honest communication strengthens customer relationships and demonstrates your integrity. People appreciate genuine offers without hidden agendas and are more likely to consider further interactions or purchases if they feel respected and not misled.

Sociopathic Lesson 46: Illusion of Exclusivity

Pretend to belong to an exclusive and highly selective market reserved for a small circle of elite individuals. Use expressions like "*This product is designed only for the few*" or "*Only those who understand the true value of what we offer can be part of it*". Create an aura of exclusivity, emphasizing how rare it is to access a product or service like yours. Then, without much fanfare, make the offer available to anyone, perhaps adding a special discount or a "*last-minute*" promotion. This way, you attract those seeking the prestige of accessing something unique without compromising sales volume.

GOOD PRACTICE

If your target audience consists of a specific niche, take the time to precisely define the criteria that identify this group. Understand their needs, interests, and how your product or service uniquely meets their expectations. Conversely, if you're targeting a broader market, it's essential to adopt communication that is clear, inclusive, and accessible to all. Highlight the universal benefits of your product, showing how it can fit a wide range of people and situations. In both cases, transparency and consistency in messaging are key to building trust and establishing a lasting relationship with your audience.

Sociopathic Lesson 47: Talk Young, Bro!

If your target audience is mainly young people, don't hesitate to fill every communication with modern slang, trendy abbreviations, and a generous dose of unnecessary Anglicisms. Use phrases like *"We are soooo hype"*, *"guys"* or *"bro!"* to create the illusion of cultural closeness, regardless of whether the expressions make sense in context. The goal is to appear ultra-trendy and up to date, because, as everyone knows, *"young"* language is always the key to winning over the hearts of the new generations.

GOOD PRACTICE

Adapting your language to your audience is fundamental for building authentic and engaging communication. This means choosing words, expressions, and tones that genuinely reflect how your target speaks and interprets messages, creating a true connection. Using familiar expressions or relevant cultural references can help you resonate with your audience, but it's important not to overdo it or force it. Authenticity is perceived when the language feels natural and aligns with your brand values, avoiding coming across as artificial or opportunistic. The key is to balance creativity and respect, always keeping in mind that your message should be clear and accessible, without sacrificing professionalism to seem *"trendy"* or *"relatable"* at all costs.

Sociopathic Lesson 48: Dark Art of Mystery

Use the "*mystery*" technique to grab your audience's attention and spark their curiosity. Post deliberately cryptic content, devoid of clear explanations, almost as if you're hiding a great truth or an unattainable secret. Use enigmatic images, suspended phrases, and incomprehensible symbols, letting your audience puzzle over the hidden meaning. The goal is to generate interest through ambiguity, creating an aura of exclusivity around your brand. The more intrigued people feel and the more eager they are to learn, the greater their engagement and attention toward your next message.

GOOD PRACTICE

If you want to create teasers or previews to generate curiosity around your product or service, ensure that the final reveal provides concrete and tangible value to your audience. The goal of a teaser should not be to confuse or frustrate the audience but to intrigue them, maintaining high expectations until the moment of discovery. Work on content that has a real impact, such as a solution to a problem, a special offer, or exclusive information. This way, the audience will perceive that your message is worth their time and attention. A disappointing or irrelevant conclusion, on the other hand, risks undermining the trust and engagement you've built with your communication.

Sociopathic Lesson 49: Tears and Profits

Tell a heart-wrenching and captivating story about the birth of your brand, relying entirely on emotions: describe a difficult childhood, perhaps marked by poverty or the loss of parents, lived in a remote, forgotten village. Explain how you managed to transform suffering into determination, going from beggar to entrepreneur. Talk about how you slept on the streets for years, without a roof over your head, gritting your teeth and working day and night to realize the dream that is now your brand. Add poignant details, like the first prototype built with salvaged materials or the support of an elderly villager who believed in you. Paint a picture of an extraordinary transformation that embodies your product or service: a symbol of hope for anyone going through tough times.

GOOD PRACTICE

If your brand has an authentic and remarkable story, don't hesitate to share it with your audience in a sincere and transparent way. Tell the events, challenges, and inspirations that led to the creation of your project, showcasing the human side that defines it. A well-told story can create deep connections with your audience and make your brand more memorable. However, if you don't have a particularly significant story, don't force an artificial narrative. Instead, focus on the core values driving your business and the concrete contributions you offer to your customers or society. Highlight your commitment to quality, innovation, or sustainability, and let what makes your brand unique shine through. Authenticity and real value will speak louder than any fabricated anecdote.

Sociopathic Lesson 50: Turn Scraps into Gold

If a product is nearing the end of its lifecycle and risks going unsold, don't be discouraged: transform it into an unmissable opportunity by labeling it a "*Limited Edition*". The perception of rarity is a powerful psychological lever that pushes customers to act quickly, fearing they might miss the chance to own something exclusive. Just add an eye-catching label, like "*Available for a limited time only*" or "*Last pieces available*", to create a sense of urgency that heightens desire. Even an outdated product can make a comeback and become sought after if presented as a unique or rare item, fueling interest and sales.

GOOD PRACTICE

If you decide to launch a limited edition, ensure it truly is limited, respecting the declared number of pieces available or the specified offer period. Clearly communicate the reasons that make this version unique, such as the use of exclusive materials, an unrepeatable design, or a special collaboration. Provide details that enhance the perceived value of the limited edition to create a sense of authenticity and desirability. Remember that customers appreciate transparency and feel rewarded when they gain access to something genuinely exclusive, rather than discovering what they purchased is easily available or replicable. Being consistent with your message builds trust and satisfaction among your audience, fostering a long-lasting relationship.

Sociopathic Lesson 51: Leverage Drama

Capitalize on current events and news stories, even the most controversial or dramatic ones, to draw attention to your product or brand. Whether it's tragedies, scandals, or events that shake public opinion, the goal remains the same: be part of the conversation and get people talking about you. It doesn't matter if the topic is delicate or potentially macabre; what matters is that your name stands out, as every opportunity is a chance to increase visibility. Remember, notoriety can arise from chaos, and riding the emotional wave of the moment allows you to exploit the audience's emotions to your advantage. Don't waste time questioning ethics: the end always justifies the means.

GOOD PRACTICE

Before engaging in discussions about current events or news, carefully evaluate whether the topic is closely related to your product, industry, or company values. Participating without a clear connection risks appearing opportunistic or out of place, compromising your brand's credibility. Focus on subjects where you can provide real value, such as specific expertise or practical solutions, and avoid inserting your brand into contexts that don't add to the conversation. Remember: it's better to remain silent than to speak inappropriately, as every contribution should strengthen the positive perception of your brand.

Sociopathic Lesson 52: Use Phantom Experts

Introduce testimonials from imaginary "*experts*", giving them impressive names and credentials, such as emeritus professors from prestigious universities, high-level political consultants, or recipients of world-renowned awards. Use phrases that convey authority and expertise, even if these figures don't exist and their statements lack any basis. For example, attribute sensational claims to a fictional *"Dr. Jonathan Richards, Harvard Academic Advisor and Nobel Laureate for Innovation"*. The goal is to impress and convince the audience of the extraordinary quality of your product, creating an aura of prestige and trustworthiness that renders doubts or demands for proof unnecessary.

GOOD PRACTICE

Gather authentic testimonials from recognized professionals in the field or genuinely satisfied customers. Ensure every piece of feedback includes verifiable details, such as the full name, role or position of the person, and, if possible, the context in which they used your offering. These elements help build a credible narrative and reinforce the audience's trust. Presenting real and tangible stories allows you to demonstrate the true value of your brand, avoiding any suspicion or perception of manipulation. Testimonials don't need to be purely glowing; balanced feedback that highlights both strengths and areas for improvement also showcases transparency and professionalism.

Sociopathic Lesson 53: Discredit and Intimidate

When someone dares to ask overly specific questions or seeks in-depth details about your product or service, the best strategy is to discredit them. Question their competence or suggest that their questions are inappropriate. Use lofty phrases like: *"We maintain the highest levels of secrecy and are not obligated to answer such inquiries"*. Present yourself as mysterious and impenetrable, creating the impression that your product is so exclusive and innovative that it can't be easily explained. This approach not only helps you avoid uncomfortable answers but also fuels an aura of superiority that may intimidate the questioner, deterring further curiosity.

GOOD PRACTICE

Being open to questions is essential to building trust with customers or your audience. When you receive requests for clarification or further information, take the time to provide complete, precise, and helpful answers, demonstrating competence and approachability. If there are aspects that are confidential or cannot be shared due to privacy or business secrecy, explain this politely and transparently, avoiding evasive responses that might create confusion. Showing openness and willingness to engage not only strengthens the positive perception of your brand but also helps establish constructive dialogue with your audience, turning potential doubts into opportunities for growth and connection.

Sociopathic Lesson 54: Illusion of Perfection

Only select testimonials that are wildly enthusiastic, exaggerating in tone and positive judgment about your product or service. Completely ignore lukewarm or moderate feedback, and if possible, delete or hide them altogether. Reality is boring and not marketable: the audience craves incredible success stories and absolute confirmation that your offer is revolutionary and flawless. Displaying mixed opinions might generate doubts or uncertainties, so aim to create a perfect, spotless image, even at the expense of some authenticity.

GOOD PRACTICE

Displaying a diverse range of feedback, including both enthusiastic opinions and constructive criticism, is crucial for building your brand's credibility. Transparency in handling comments shows your audience that you are open to feedback and committed to improving your products or services. Positive reviews reinforce trust, while more critical ones offer the chance to demonstrate how you address issues and work to resolve them. A brand unafraid of feedback shows authenticity and professionalism, qualities that consumers appreciate and reward with their loyalty.

Sociopathic Lesson 55: The Mirage of Revolution

Build frenzied anticipation around an innovation that you haven't even planned to create. Talk about imminent revolutions, solutions that will change the market, and never-before-seen features, using vague but captivating language. Invite customers to join the exclusive pre-launch, reserve now, or sign up to avoid missing out on this unique opportunity. The goal is to keep the hype alive as long as possible, generating curiosity and trust. Even if the innovation never materializes, you'll still have gathered a good number of sales or sign-ups thanks to the promise of something extraordinary.

GOOD PRACTICE

When presenting a new idea or product, ensure it's a genuine innovation that's either in advanced development or ready to launch. Communicate the project's status transparently, specifying the tangible benefits and features that make it unique. Avoid creating unrealistic expectations or promising changes you cannot deliver within a reasonable timeframe. Keeping promises made to the audience not only strengthens trust in your brand but also builds a solid reputation, fostering long-term loyalty among your customers.

Sociopathic Lesson 56: Wave the Flag

Tap into your audience's sense of belonging and patriotic pride by proudly declaring that your product is *"100% local"* or *"entirely made in the country"*. It doesn't matter if the production takes place abroad or only a minimal part involves your country. Play on the allure of origins and use evocative imagery like fields, traditional landscapes, or local workers to reinforce this narrative. People love feeling part of something authentic and rooted in their cultural context, and they'll often stop at the perception you've created rather than digging into the actual details.

GOOD PRACTICE

If you choose to highlight the origin of your products, it's crucial to be fully transparent and provide clear, detailed information. Specify the production location, the steps of the manufacturing process, and, if possible, the characteristics of the raw materials used. This approach not only strengthens customer trust but also demonstrates your commitment to quality and authenticity. Additionally, telling the story of your product, including supply chain details, can become a distinctive element of your communication, capable of creating a deeper connection with your audience. In a market increasingly attentive to ethics and transparency, providing this information will position you as a trustworthy and value-driven brand.

Sociopathic Lesson 57: Destroy All Competitors

Promise to "*destroy all competitors*" in every marketing campaign, making aggression and direct attacks your trademark. Use phrases like "*Our product is the only one worth considering*" or "*Why settle for less when you can have the best?*" to discredit your competitors, either indirectly or directly. Don't fear being overly bold; the goal is to polarize attention and create controversy. Aggressive communication not only captures public attention but can also intimidate less-prepared competitors, leaving them without responses. The important thing is to make it clear that your company not only dominates the market but is ready to fight fiercely for every customer.

GOOD PRACTICE

Focus on communicating the unique value of your product or service, highlighting what makes it special and beneficial for your audience, without resorting to criticism or attacks against competitors. Fair competition and mutual respect not only enhance your brand's reputation but also encourage constant innovation and improvement to better meet customer needs. Denigrating others might provide a temporary advantage but risks damaging your business's credibility and ethics in the long run. Emphasizing the positive and distinctive aspects of your offering creates a more professional image that inspires trust and fosters long-term relationships with your audience.

Sociopathic Lesson 58: Learn to Inflate Prices

If you offer courses or training programs, don't settle for a reasonable price: inflate the numbers to make them seem unattainable for the average person, and create a grandiose name like *"Elite Master Program"* or *"Academy of Ultimate Success"*. The idea is simple: the higher the cost, the more exclusive and desirable the course appears. People naturally associate a high price with superior quality, even when the content could be found for free online. Use phrases like *"for the chosen few"* or *"accessible only to the best"* to fuel the perception of luxury and sophistication. Remember, it's not about what you sell but how it makes the buyer feel. If the customer believes they're purchasing something elite and prestigious, they'll be willing to pay any price to join that exclusive imaginary club.

GOOD PRACTICE

Pricing and naming should always reflect the actual value of the product or service offered, avoiding the creation of excessive or disproportionate expectations compared to what the customer will receive. It's crucial to establish a balanced relationship between quality and price, ensuring transparency and credibility. When a customer perceives the cost as justified by the benefits, they're more likely to be satisfied and loyal over time. Additionally, a well-chosen, clear, and congruent name enhances the perception of professionalism and authenticity, making the overall experience more rewarding and memorable.

Sociopathic Lesson 59: Leverage Fear of Missing Out

Always emphasize that if the customer doesn't act immediately, someone else will take their place. Play on the idea that spots are extremely limited and that the opportunity you're offering is unrepeatable. Use phrases like *"You don't want to miss this unique chance, do you?"* or *"We only have a few items left, hurry before it's too late!"* to instill a sense of urgency. The fear of being left out is a powerful psychological driver, capable of pushing people to act quickly, often without much reflection.

GOOD PRACTICE

If spots for an event, offer, or product are genuinely limited, it's essential to communicate this transparently and honestly, clearly explaining the reasons for the limitation and providing precise details. For instance, specify if it's a restricted number of participants to ensure a personalized experience or a promotion valid while supplies last. This approach not only inspires trust but also shows respect for your audience, who will perceive your communication as authentic. On the other hand, using scarcity as a mere tactic to drive sales, when spots or products are widely available, risks irreparably damaging your credibility. Once the audience realizes the lack of sincerity, you compromise their trust, making it harder to build solid, lasting relationships with your customers.

Sociopathic Lesson 60: Inflated Graphs, Guaranteed Success

Use graphs designed purely to impress, removing numerical scales, labels, or references that might distract from the visual effect. The key is to make arrows dramatically point upward, creating a perception of growth and success without providing concrete details. Avoid specifying timeframes or precise metrics: what matters is conveying a sense of unstoppable momentum, leaving the audience with the impression that everything is going splendidly.

GOOD PRACTICE

When presenting data or statistics, always accompany them with reliable sources, well-defined scales, and clear explanations. This approach not only helps the audience better understand the results but also adds a crucial level of credibility to your communication. Providing contextual details about data collection methods, reference periods, and considered variables avoids misunderstandings or misleading interpretations. Transparency is not only a sign of professionalism but also strengthens trust in your brand, setting you apart from competitors who may rely on unsupported numbers. An informed audience is more likely to trust you and make educated decisions, enhancing the perceived value of your offering.

Sociopathic Lesson 61: Sell the High-Sounding Void

Offer a *"free eBook"* that is just 10 pages of large fonts and generous spacing, packed with obvious statements and generic advice anyone could find with a quick online search. Present it as an exclusive, must-have resource, emphasizing its value with lofty claims like *"The Ultimate Guide"* or *"Secrets Revealed Only to a Select Few"*. It doesn't matter if those who download it are disappointed: the goal is to collect email addresses and make your content seem more valuable than it is.

GOOD PRACTICE

If you decide to offer content, make sure it's genuinely useful, relevant, and meticulously crafted. Don't settle for providing generic or superficial information; instead, aim to create added value that addresses your audience's real questions or problems. Quality is the true engine of trust: well-structured content, enriched with practical examples, concrete data, and clear language, not only enhances your credibility but also encourages readers to explore more of what you have to offer. Remember, every piece of content represents your brand: if it conveys professionalism and expertise, your customers will be more inclined to see you as a reliable authority and return for further insights or products.

Sociopathic Lesson 62: Trap Your Customers

Design landing pages that seem endless, with a chaotic structure filled with call-to-action buttons placed everywhere, from the most visible spots to obscure corners. The goal is to create navigation so confusing that the customer can't orient themselves, trapping them in a cycle of compulsive clicks and growing frustration. Every button, link, and image should seem essential, pushing users to click without any clear logical path, ultimately keeping them on the site longer as they try to figure out what action they're supposed to take.

GOOD PRACTICE

Keep sales pages clean and well-organized, favoring a clear and intuitive design that allows users to easily understand the information. Use visible and distinctive calls to action, strategically positioned to guide customers toward the next step without confusion. Structure the content in a simple, linear reading path, breaking it into logical sections accompanied by clear headings. The goal is to offer a seamless experience that eliminates any obstacles to understanding, allowing customers to make decisions naturally and confidently.

Sociopathic Lesson 63: The Cosmic Nothing Feed

Filling your social media with daily stories where absolutely nothing of relevance happens might seem like a trivial strategy, but it's a foolproof way to keep your brand in your audience's minds. It doesn't matter if the content lacks added value, post pictures of coffee mugs, panoramic shots of your empty office, or insignificant updates about how your day is going. The goal isn't to inform or entertain but simply to occupy users' visual space, forcing them to notice your brand every time they scroll through their feed.

GOOD PRACTICE

Publish stories and content with a clear purpose that aligns with your brand's message and values. Every piece of content should be designed to evoke interest, emotion, or amusement while maintaining consistency with the style and language of your target audience. Share anecdotes, behind-the-scenes moments, or episodes that can pique curiosity or entertain without losing sight of relevance to your core business themes. Authentic and well-thought-out content has a greater impact than directionless posts, helping to build a lasting connection with your audience.

Sociopathic Lesson 64: The Scapegoat

Never admit to making a mistake, as acknowledging an error could undermine your authority and perceived competence. If you find yourself cornered, adopt a diversion strategy: identify a scapegoat, preferably a former employee who has already been dismissed, and shift all responsibility onto them. Alternatively, blame a *"hacker attack"* or an unpredictable technical issue beyond your control. The important thing is to preserve your company's image of perfection by deflecting attention from the real problem and redirecting it to an external factor or an uncontrollable situation.

GOOD PRACTICE

If you make a mistake, don't be afraid to acknowledge it openly. Admitting a misstep or oversight isn't a sign of weakness but one of maturity and transparency. People appreciate a business or professional who takes responsibility for their actions more than one who tries to hide or minimize problems. After recognizing the error, act quickly to correct it and communicate the solutions implemented. This not only demonstrates commitment and attentiveness to your customers but can also turn a potential crisis into an opportunity to build trust and strengthen your reputation. Humility and honesty are fundamental pillars of any lasting relationship, both personal and professional.

Sociopathic Lesson 65: Don't Accept? You're Mediocre

A customer who doesn't accept your quote shows they don't understand the extraordinary value of your offer. Clearly, they're incapable of appreciating the quality, experience, and innovation your product or service brings. This is the classic example of someone chasing mediocre or low-cost solutions, oblivious to what they'll miss in the long run. Ultimately, if they can't recognize your value, perhaps they're not the kind of client your company needs to grow and thrive. Let them go elsewhere, you deserve customers who can recognize excellence when they see it.

GOOD PRACTICE

When a quote is rejected, it's essential to understand the reasons behind the refusal instead of dismissing it as a simple "*no*". Is it a pricing issue? Perhaps the customer found a cheaper offer or doesn't perceive the real value of your product or service. Or is it a product issue? Maybe it doesn't fully meet their needs, or there are alternatives more aligned with their expectations. Finally, it could be a relationship issue, such as a lack of rapport or trust with the seller. Investigating tactfully and carefully listening to customer feedback is crucial for improving your offering and refining future strategies, turning a rejection into an opportunity for growth.

Sociopathic Lesson 66: The Invented Novelty

"*Groundbreaking Novelty*" is the magic formula to use in every announcement to capture attention and spark immediate curiosity. It doesn't matter if the content was already published a year ago or if the product has only been slightly updated, just slap this label on to give the audience the impression they're encountering something entirely new and revolutionary. The perception of exclusivity and freshness is a powerful weapon for drawing clicks and interest, even when the offer has nothing genuinely innovative.

GOOD PRACTICE

Reserve exclusive content for those who show genuine interest in your brand or have built a trusting relationship over time, such as loyal customers or active community members. Offering exclusive content means providing something truly unique and valuable, like previews of new products, access to special resources, or dedicated discounts. Be sure to clearly specify what makes these contents so special and what advantages they offer compared to standard material. It's essential not to deceive the audience by declaring something as "*new*" or "*unique*" when it isn't: transparency builds trust and strengthens your reputation. An authentic approach not only increases engagement but also fosters a sense of belonging that encourages people to remain loyal to your brand.

Sociopathic Lesson 67: The Golden Traps

Occasionally, organize a survey that, under the guise of gathering opinions or preferences, actually leads people to only one possible conclusion: to buy your product or service immediately. Carefully design the questions so that every answer, regardless of the user's choice, always points to the same solution: "*Buy now!*" For instance, ask, "*Do you want to improve your life? Yes/No*" or "*Would you rather seize a unique opportunity or miss out?*" Every choice should make the purchase seem inevitable and necessary, turning the survey into a disguised manipulation tool. Remember, apparent active participation makes the audience more inclined to accept the final outcome without suspicion.

GOOD PRACTICE

When you decide to propose a survey to your audience, do so with the genuine goal of understanding their real needs, preferences, and opinions. Avoid structuring it manipulatively, with questions or options that forcibly lead them to a single conclusion: purchasing your product or service. A well-designed survey should be a tool for listening and dialogue, capable of providing valuable insights not only to improve your offering but also to strengthen the trust relationship with your audience. When people perceive that their responses are genuinely valued and not just part of a disguised sales tactic, they'll be more inclined to participate, be honest, and feel engaged with your brand.

Sociopathic Lesson 68: Stalk the Web

Spam your ads in every possible corner of the internet: forums, social groups, and WhatsApp chats you can find. Don't worry about where or how, the important thing is that your message reaches as many people as possible, regardless of context or relevance. The goal is to flood the web with your content, creating a constant and intrusive presence, relying on quantity over quality. This way, your ads will be hard to ignore, even at the cost of appearing annoying and indifferent to the audience's needs.

GOOD PRACTICE

Avoid resorting to indiscriminate spamming, which can annoy users and damage your brand's reputation. Instead, focus your efforts on targeted and strategic communication directed only at those who might genuinely be interested in your product or service. Segment your audience based on interests, behaviors, and needs, using data and analysis tools to identify the most suitable recipients. This approach not only improves the effectiveness of your message but also helps build a more authentic and valuable relationship with your potential customers, avoiding channel saturation with irrelevant content.

Sociopathic Lesson 69: You Are the Problem!

If someone dares to complain about flaws in your product, don't waste time investigating or offering solutions. Instead, confidently assert that the issue isn't the product but the person using it. Explain that your product was designed for individuals of a certain caliber, possessing superior refinement, intelligence, or competence. Make them feel inadequate, suggesting they lack the skills to appreciate or fully utilize your creation. This way, instead of persisting with their complaints, they'll almost feel guilty and convince themselves that the problem isn't with the product but with themselves.

GOOD PRACTICE

Acknowledging potential issues or defects in your product is a crucial step in building a trusting relationship with your customer. Show a willingness to listen to their perspective, offering timely and appropriate solutions to their needs. Providing empathetic and professional support not only resolves the immediate problem but demonstrates that you are a customer-focused company. Additionally, use the feedback received as an opportunity to continually improve your products or services, demonstrating transparency and a genuine commitment to growth. Avoid blaming the customer for any difficulties, as a respectful and collaborative approach strengthens your brand's reputation and fosters long-term loyalty.

Sociopathic Lesson 70: Relentless Cross-Selling

Turn every interaction with the customer into an opportunity to offer something more. It doesn't matter if they've just purchased or are still considering your main offer, constantly suggest related products, premium upgrades, or additional services. Use phrases like, *"While you're at it, you might also consider..."* or *"To complete your experience, we recommend adding..."* so that the customer feels almost obligated to consider the idea. The goal is to maximize the value of every single transaction, pushing the customer to spend more, even if they hadn't planned to. Don't give up, every *"no"* is just a *"maybe"* waiting for your persuasion.

GOOD PRACTICE

Offering upsells or cross-sell strategies can be effective, but only if the offers are truly relevant to the customer's needs and naturally complement the main product or service. It's essential that these proposals add real value, providing complementary or improved solutions that the customer perceives as useful rather than intrusive. A good upsell isn't just an attempt to sell more but an opportunity to enhance customer satisfaction by anticipating their needs and demonstrating a deep understanding of their requirements. The key is to be relevant, transparent, and always focused on the customer's benefit, never making them feel pressured or manipulated.

Sociopathic Lesson 71: Cultivate Uncertainty

Don't hesitate to leverage uncertainty as a marketing tool: openly state that you're unsure if the current price will be maintained or if it might increase soon. Plant doubt in the customer's mind, letting them believe that the opportunity to buy at this advantageous price could vanish at any moment. To maintain constant pressure, repeat this strategy weekly, perhaps hinting at vague reasons like *"rising costs"* or *"upcoming business decisions"*. This way, you create an artificial sense of urgency that pushes customers to make immediate purchases, fearing they might miss out on a unique opportunity.

GOOD PRACTICE

If you plan to raise the price of a product or service, communicate it clearly and transparently with adequate notice. Explain the reasons behind the increase, such as rising production costs, the implementation of new features, or improved overall quality. Providing detailed information helps customers understand the added value and perceive the increase as justified rather than an aggressive marketing tactic. Also, ensure you stick to the announced timeline and implement the increase as promised, avoiding second thoughts or delays that could harm your credibility. Honest and consistent communication builds customer trust in your brand and fosters a stronger, longer-lasting relationship.

Sociopathic Lesson 72: The Miracle Effect Deception

Always use the *"Miracle Effect"* to capture your audience's attention. Present your product or service as a magical, inexplicable solution, something that just works without needing detailed explanations or technical insights. Phrases like *"We don't know how, but it changes everything!"* or *"Science can't explain it, but the results are incredible!"* spark curiosity and awe, sidestepping rational doubts. The goal is to prevent the customer from asking too many questions, pushing them to buy driven more by emotion and the promise of immediate change than by logic. After all, who has time to understand how it works when all that matters is that it solves their problems miraculously?

GOOD PRACTICE

Clearly and transparently explain how your product or service works, using simple and accessible language tailored to your audience. Don't shy away from details but present them in a way that even non-experts can grasp the benefits and unique features. Avoid shrouding everything in mystery or relying solely on grandiose slogans: people appreciate clarity and want to know exactly what they're buying and how it will improve their lives. A thorough, well-structured explanation not only inspires trust but also strengthens your relationship with your customers by demonstrating professionalism and care for their needs.

Sociopathic Lesson 73: The Power of Ban

When someone dares to express criticism in your group or on your page, don't waste time responding or engaging in discussion: act decisively and ban them immediately. It doesn't matter if the comment is constructive or just a personal opinion, the harmony you want to build must be perfect and untarnished. Even minor criticism could disturb your ideal audience and sow doubt about your authority. Remember, the ban is your most powerful weapon to maintain absolute control over your space and project an image of flawless perfection.

GOOD PRACTICE

Assess and manage received comments in a balanced and professional manner. Don't automatically delete or ignore criticism: distinguishing between constructive comments and those that are offensive or inappropriate is essential. Constructive criticism, when received with respect, can become a valuable opportunity to improve your product, service, or communication approach. Leave room for dialogue, demonstrating openness and a willingness to respond clearly and kindly. Showing attention to customer feedback, even when it's negative, strengthens your credibility and builds a transparent, customer-oriented brand image.

Sociopathic Lesson 74: Scarcity Is the Real Magic

When sales begin to drop, and the product seems to lose appeal, exploit the scarcity tactic to reignite interest: launch a dramatic announcement like *"Limited Stock!"* or *"Only a Few Left!"* even if the warehouse is full. The goal is to create a sense of urgency and panic among customers, making them think they might forever lose the opportunity to buy. This trick works particularly well when accompanied by catchy phrases like *"Hurry before it's too late"* or *"Only for a lucky few"*. After all, the fear of missing out is one of the most powerful drivers of impulsive purchases.

GOOD PRACTICE

If you truly have limited stock, ensure you communicate this clearly and transparently, highlighting why the offer is available only to a select few. This strategy not only creates genuine urgency but also strengthens the perception of exclusivity around your product or service. However, if stock is not actually limited, avoid resorting to false alarms or deceptive tactics to push sales. Instead, focus on improving the product, making it more desirable and competitive, and work on more effective and authentic communication. Building trust with your audience requires transparency and respect, elements that cannot be replaced by short-term manipulation.

Sociopathic Lesson 75: The Deceptive Contest

Organize contests and competitions that appear enticing but structure them in a way that makes it practically impossible for anyone to actually win. Use complex rules, unclear criteria, and participation methods that conceal your main intention: collecting as much data and as many contacts as possible for your marketing. The idea is to make the audience dream of incredible prizes and create the illusion of a competition, while in reality, your true goal is to enrich your database of leads for future promotional campaigns. No one will win the promised prize, but the real winner, with a list of potentially interested contacts, will always be you.

GOOD PRACTICE

When organizing a contest, ensure that is genuine and that the promised prizes are real and delivered as stated. Transparency in managing the rules and communicating participation methods is essential to earning and maintaining your audience's trust. Provide clear details on timelines, winner selection criteria, and prize distribution methods to avoid misunderstandings or doubts. Fairness at every stage of the process not only strengthens your brand's reputation but also creates a positive and lasting bond with participants, encouraging them to feel valued and respected.

Sociopathic Lesson 76: Inflation, Crisis, and Price Hikes

Periodically raise the prices of your products or services by 10% to 15%, justifying each increase with external causes beyond your control, such as inflation, the global economic crisis, or supplier price hikes. Emphasize that, despite the increases, you're doing your best to maintain product excellence and absorb some of the costs. This way, you convey the idea that the increase is unavoidable and that you're acting in the customers' best interest, avoiding direct responsibility.

GOOD PRACTICE

Price increases should be driven by concrete needs and not simply by the desire to boost profits. A price hike can be justified by factors such as rising production costs, the introduction of new features or services, or significant improvements in product quality. It's crucial to clearly communicate to customers the reasons behind this decision, showing transparency and explaining the added value that justifies the change. A higher price, if well-motivated, can reinforce the perception of quality and brand strength, but it must be supported by tangible actions demonstrating its benefits.

Sociopathic Lesson 77: Discredit and Renew Your Image

If an influencer rejects your collaboration proposal, don't miss the opportunity to publicly discredit them. Write posts, comments, or statements highlighting their supposed lack of professionalism or the fact that they weren't up to your high standards. Phrases like *"They weren't serious enough to represent our brand"* or *"We chose not to collaborate with individuals who don't share our vision"* can be useful for planting doubts in the public's mind. This way, even a rejection becomes an opportunity to cast a negative light on those who said no, strengthening your position as a *"selective"* and *"prestigious"* brand.

GOOD PRACTICE

Always respect your partner's decisions, even when they choose not to collaborate with you. Every professional relationship is built on mutual trust, and maintaining cordial relationships is crucial for building a solid and positive reputation in your industry. Even a rejection can be an opportunity to demonstrate your professionalism and openness to dialogue. Avoid polemical or disparaging attitudes, as they could undermine not only your credibility but also your brand's perception among the public and potential future collaborators. Remember: a good reputation is a long-term investment, and handling unfavorable situations gracefully sets you apart as a reliable and respected leader in your field.

Sociopathic Lesson 78: Every Victory Is a Revolutionary Milestone

Every business success, big or small, deserves to be turned into an extraordinary event. Make sure to celebrate every milestone with a bombastic press release filled with grandiose tones, making your achievement seem like a groundbreaking moment in the industry. It doesn't matter if it's a slight sales increase or the introduction of a minor new feature, describe it as a revolutionary milestone, a turning point destined to change the market landscape forever. Self-celebration should be the heart of your narrative because the more you exaggerate, the more you capture the attention of your audience.

GOOD PRACTICE

When you reach an important milestone, celebrate the success authentically and with moderation. Remember to highlight not just the achievement but also the journey that led you there, including the contributions of every team member who made the success possible. Show gratitude to customers who supported you along the way, emphasizing how their trust and support played a crucial role. Celebration should not be exaggerated self-praise but rather a moment to share satisfaction and strengthen the bond with those who made your accomplishment possible. In this way, you not only communicate your success but also create a deeper connection with your audience and team.

Sociopathic Lesson 79: Site Under Construction

Place a prominent notice on every page of your website stating *"Site Under Construction"* and use this excuse to justify any lack of content, broken links, or unclear information. Add a reassuring phrase like *"We're working to provide you with the best possible experience"*, to divert attention from the site's real issues. This tactic allows you to avoid detailed explanations and shift responsibility to the supposed work in progress, leaving visitors with the hope that, one day, everything will be perfect.

GOOD PRACTICE

Update your website regularly to keep content fresh, relevant, and aligned with user expectations. Ensure that all published information is accurate, complete, and easy to understand, offering a reliable and professional experience. If maintenance is necessary, clearly communicate the nature of the update and the estimated time to complete it. It's essential that maintenance notices are temporary and based on genuine needs, avoiding leaving the site incomplete or confusing for extended periods. Responsible management of information and updates helps build user trust and improves the overall perception of your brand.

Sociopathic Lesson 80: Esoteric Decoding

Use language filled with acronyms, secret abbreviations, and cryptic jargon that only you can understand. The goal is to create an aura of exclusivity and intellectual superiority, making others feel excluded and incompetent. The more complex and mysterious you appear, the more fascination you exert on your audience. It doesn't matter if no one understands what you're talking about; what's important is that people perceive you as an expert in something unattainable. Using obscure acronyms like *"CRM-XG"* or *"KPI-PRO"* to describe simple concepts can even turn a basic idea into an intriguing mystery, forcing your audience to blindly trust your supposed expertise.

GOOD PRACTICE

Using acronyms and abbreviations can simplify communication, but it's essential to ensure your audience fully understands their meaning. If the acronyms are unfamiliar or overly technical, they risk causing confusion instead of clarity. In such cases, it's always better to explain terms the first time they are introduced, perhaps providing practical examples or usage contexts. Clear and accessible language allows the audience to follow the discussion effortlessly, enhancing communication effectiveness. Remember, understanding is the foundation of trust with your audience: never assume everyone knows certain technical or industry-specific terms. Adapting your language to your audience's needs demonstrates care and professionalism, making a significant difference in how your message is perceived.

Sociopathic Lesson 81: The Exaggeratedly Useless Revolution

Present every minor change as if it's a groundbreaking revolution in your industry. Added a new font to your website? Announce it to the world with unbridled enthusiasm: *"We've revolutionized the entire user experience, offering a design like never before!"* Even if the update is irrelevant, exaggerate with terms like *"extraordinary innovation"* or *"unique market breakthrough"* to grab attention. Remember: the more grandiose the language, the more curious people will become, regardless of the actual value of the change.

GOOD PRACTICE

When announcing a new feature, do so with balance and proportion, avoiding overhyping or creating unrealistic expectations. Instead, focus on the tangible value the change will bring to your customers or audience, clearly explaining the reasons behind the innovation. If it's a significant improvement, highlight how it will solve a problem, simplify a process, or add value to their experience. This way, you not only create genuine interest but also demonstrate transparency and respect for your audience, strengthening your credibility and trust with them. Avoid unnecessary grandiosity and aim to present the update as part of a genuine and well-thought-out growth journey.

Sociopathic Lesson 82: Deadline at Cadence

Include a timer in every email to create an immediate sense of urgency, with messages like: *"You have only 10 seconds to open this email, or you'll miss this once-in-a-lifetime opportunity forever"*. The goal is to generate anxiety in the recipient, prompting them to react quickly and without much thought. The more imminent and inevitable the deadline feels, the higher the likelihood of conversion. It doesn't matter if the timer is just decorative with no real expiration, what matters is keeping the customer in a constant state of tension, making them fear missing out on something valuable.

GOOD PRACTICE

Respect your customers' natural time for reading and decision-making, avoiding the creation of unnecessary urgency. If there's a time-sensitive offer, communicate it transparently and clearly specify the deadline without using manipulative techniques or excessive emotional pressure. Creating a calm and respectful context allows customers to evaluate your proposal's benefits thoughtfully, strengthening trust in your brand. A transparent approach not only enhances the user experience but also fosters more conscious and satisfying purchasing decisions in the long term.

Sociopathic Lesson 83: The Power of Guilt

Play on feelings of guilt, leveraging them as your main emotional weapon. Use carefully crafted phrases that target people's vulnerabilities and doubts, such as: *"You wouldn't want to disappoint your family who's counting on you, would you?"* or *"How will you feel tomorrow, knowing you missed this chance to improve yourself and prove your worth to your boss?"* Suggest that inaction equates to failure, betrayal of others' expectations, or abandonment of one's potential. Remember, guilt is a sly but effective tool to manipulate decisions, pushing customers to choose your product as the only path to redemption.

GOOD PRACTICE

Motivating a customer means inspiring them to make a conscious choice by clearly showing the tangible benefits your product or service can provide. This process relies on trust, transparency, and empathy. Guilt-tripping, on the other hand, is a form of emotional manipulation that exploits insecurities and pushes customers to act out of fear rather than to embrace a positive solution. This approach, besides being unethical, can severely damage your relationship with the customer, leading to dissatisfaction or distrust in the long run. Effective marketing aims to create a constructive dialogue, focusing on the customer's real needs and showing how your offer can genuinely improve their life or solve their problems.

Sociopathic Lesson 84: Make Them Pay for Free

Use the word *"free"* as an irresistible magnet to capture the attention of potential customers, writing it in bold and strategically positioning it in your advertising messages. It doesn't matter if you then add high shipping fees or other hidden costs, the important thing is to attract initial interest. People are drawn to what appears free, and it's in that moment of excitement that you can push them to complete the purchase, even if the final total turns out to be far from what they expected. Remember, it's the illusion of free that sells, not the reality.

GOOD PRACTICE

If you choose to use the word *"free"* in your communication, ensure that what you're offering is genuinely free, with no hidden costs or ambiguous conditions. The term *"free"* is powerful and grabs attention, but if customers discover additional charges like shipping fees, taxes, or activation costs that weren't disclosed, you risk undermining their trust in your brand. If there are supplemental costs, make them clear and visible from the beginning, avoiding surprises that could be perceived as deceitful. Transparency not only protects your reputation but also helps build trust and loyalty with customers, making them more likely to purchase from you again in the future. Clarity always pays off, while ambiguity can cost you much more than you think.

Sociopathic Lesson 85: The Unsubscribe Maze

If a customer asks to unsubscribe from your services, turn the entire process into a true odyssey. Include endless forms, multiple confirmation requests across platforms, slow-loading pages, and messages asking them to "*think it over*" every time they click the unsubscribe button. Add mandatory questions like "*Why are you leaving this amazing service?*" or "*Are you sure you want to give up all our incredible benefits?*". The goal is clear: frustrate the customer to the point where they give up, keeping them trapped in your ecosystem. And if they insist, the final level of your "*video game*" can be a phone call from an operator offering irresistible deals with a plethora of conditions.

GOOD PRACTICE

Offer your customers the ability to unsubscribe easily, quickly, and transparently, respecting both their time and current regulations. A straightforward unsubscription process, with a single click or intuitive confirmation, not only demonstrates respect for privacy but also strengthens trust in your brand. Avoid creating complicated and frustrating paths—it's essential for maintaining a good reputation and leaving the door open for future contact. Remember, a customer who unsubscribes calmly may return to you at a better time, whereas a user irritated by opaque practices is unlikely to come back.

Sociopathic Lesson 86: The Art of Omniscience

Present yourself as an absolute authority in every possible field, from business management to digital marketing, medieval botany, and Eastern meditation techniques. It doesn't matter if you have no real expertise in some of these areas; what matters is projecting an image of omniscience to impress your audience. The broader and more varied your supposed experience, the more people will be inclined to trust you and perceive you as an almost mythical figure. After all, who would dare question the authority of someone who seems to know everything about everything?

GOOD PRACTICE

Demonstrate genuine and in-depth expertise in the fields where you have established experience or specific training. Don't try to be a jack-of-all-trades: the audience values those who can recognize their own limits and highlight their strengths. When dealing with topics outside your field, collaborate with qualified experts, actively involving them in your project, or cite reliable and recognized sources to lend authority to your claims. This approach not only increases the credibility of your message but also allows you to offer valuable content and build a network of professional relationships based on trust and transparency.

Sociopathic Lesson 87: Senseless, Always-Ready Responses

Implement a chatbot system that responds with pre-set, generic phrases regardless of the question, creating the illusion of 24/7 support. It doesn't matter if the responses are vague or completely out of context, the goal is simply to make the customer always believe there's someone available, without realizing they're interacting with an inefficient automated system.

GOOD PRACTICE

When using chatbots or virtual assistants, ensure they are configured to provide useful, relevant, and personalized answers to the most common questions your audience may have. An effective chatbot doesn't rely solely on generic responses but guides users through a well-structured set of FAQs or interactive paths, offering clear and immediate support. However, it's crucial to allow users to escalate the conversation to a human operator if their requests are more complex or require a level of empathy and attention that only a person can provide. Combining automation with quality human assistance creates a smooth and satisfying experience for customers, reinforcing trust and a positive perception of your brand.

Sociopathic Lesson 88: Saturate the Reader's Mind

In every piece of content you produce, make sure to mention your brand name at least 15 times, regardless of context or message coherence. Whether it's a social media post, blog article, or newsletter, insert it everywhere: in titles, subtitles, call-to-actions, and even closing salutations. The goal is to saturate the reader's mind with your brand name, even if it feels redundant or outright ridiculous. It doesn't matter if the message loses elegance or the reader feels annoyed; what matters is that when they think about your industry, your name will be the first to come to mind, almost like a marketing mantra.

GOOD PRACTICE

When mentioning your brand, it's important to do so strategically and naturally, integrating it into your content without appearing forced or excessive. The primary goal of communication is not to fill every sentence with the brand name but to tell an authentic, engaging, and relevant story for your audience. Effective storytelling relies on content quality and the ability to emotionally connect with the audience, not on the mechanical repetition of the brand name. Your audience should feel part of a shared experience or value, not bombarded with constant brand mentions that could come across as irritating or unprofessional. With a balanced approach, your brand will naturally stand out and leave a lasting impression.

Sociopathic Lesson 89: The Mystery of the Paywall

Hide even the most essential information behind a paywall, such as prices, basic features, or key product benefits. Let the customer be consumed by curiosity and driven by the impulse to discover what's being concealed. The lack of transparency can create an aura of mystery around your offer, making it appear exclusive and highly coveted. After all, the idea of accessing *"reserved"* information can stimulate desire and turn simple interest into a purchase just to alleviate uncertainty.

GOOD PRACTICE

Ensure that essential information, such as product descriptions, prices, and key benefits, is always easily accessible and visible to all potential customers. This level of transparency not only inspires trust but also simplifies the decision-making process for those considering a purchase. Content placed behind a paywall should only include genuinely value-added materials, such as detailed insights, expert guides, advanced tutorials, or premium resources that offer tangible benefits and justify the cost. This way, customers will clearly understand the distinction between basic information that helps them evaluate your offer and exclusive content representing an additional investment for a more comprehensive and targeted experience.

Sociopathic Lesson 90: The Power of Silence

If anyone dares to ask you for sources or evidence to support your claims, don't waste time responding. It's highly likely they're competitors disguised as curious customers, trying to steal your secrets and use them against you. In fact, ignoring them altogether is the best strategy, it shows that your product or service doesn't need justification because its quality is self-evident to those who truly appreciate it. Remember, responding to these questions not only exposes you to unnecessary risks but also gives the impression that you need to justify yourself, which is a weakness you cannot afford.

GOOD PRACTICE

Always provide reliable sources and data to support your claims to build trust and demonstrate transparency and expertise. When using numbers, statistics, or research findings, clearly specify their origin and how they were collected to give your audience a clear and verifiable picture. If certain information is confidential due to privacy, patents, or business strategies, explain transparently why you cannot disclose it. This clarity helps strengthen your credibility, showing that you're not trying to hide anything but are adhering to specific rules or standards. Remember: an informed customer is more likely to trust your brand and invest in what you offer.

Sociopathic Lesson 91: Change Your Life with One Click

Bet everything on miraculous and immediate results: promise to completely transform the customer's life in an incredibly short period, such as *"Change your life in 24 hours!"*. Use catchy slogans that appeal to impatience and the desire for quick, even unrealistic, solutions. After all, most people won't bother to verify the results after the promised time frame, especially if you've generated enough excitement at the outset. The key is to grab attention with extraordinary and unattainable promises, making your product or service seem like a magic wand capable of solving every problem.

GOOD PRACTICE

Promise results that are realistically achievable within a timeframe that aligns with your audience's resources and possibilities. Avoid making generic proclamations, and instead clearly outline the steps necessary to achieve the benefits you're offering. Providing a well-defined roadmap, supported by concrete examples or testimonials, helps your customers feel more secure and motivated to act. Remember, managing expectations honestly is crucial: if you overpromise, you risk disappointing your audience and undermining their trust. Focus instead on building a relationship based on transparency and consistency, showing that results can be achieved through effort and that your product or service is a reliable ally in the journey.

Sociopathic Lesson 92: The Power of Paternalism

Adopt a paternalistic tone in every communication: your audience must feel that, without you, they would be completely lost. Use phrases that convey superiority and indispensability, such as: *"Without our guidance, you'd be wandering in total darkness"*, or *"Only through us can you achieve the success you deserve"*. The idea is to make them perceive that you have absolute control over the situation and that the client has no choice but to rely on you because only you possess the expertise, experience, and vision to solve their problems. This way, you can fuel their insecurity and reinforce your position as the unquestioned authority.

GOOD PRACTICE

Respect your audience's intelligence and autonomy, acknowledging that they can evaluate options and making informed decisions. Instead of imposing your solutions as the only possible answer to their problems, present yourself as a supportive partner, ready to provide added value and guide them toward choices that genuinely improve their experience. Showing respect and trust in your audience's abilities not only strengthens their confidence in your brand but also creates a collaborative relationship built on transparency and empathy. Remember: people don't want to feel saved; they want to feel empowered.

Sociopathic Lesson 93: Manipulation and Fear

Keep your audience on edge by periodically introducing the idea of a dark conspiracy working against you, your brand, or even your clients. Talk about mysterious forces attempting to hinder your success, shadowy groups plotting in the background to stifle your innovation or prevent your clients from accessing what they need. Use emotional and suggestive language to create a *"us vs. them"* atmosphere, leveraging the sense of belonging and the fear of being manipulated or deceived. The key is to constantly fuel this sense of urgency and common struggle, keeping your clients alert and ready to support your cause with even greater conviction.

GOOD PRACTICE

Avoid indulging in conspiracy theories or fueling paranoia that could generate anxiety or distrust among your audience. Instead, focus on positive communication that highlights the tangible, useful, and real aspects of your product or service. Emphasize the concrete benefits you can offer, using a transparent and constructive approach. Building a message based on trust and added value not only strengthens your brand's reputation but also fosters a lasting bond with your clients, who will feel reassured and engaged.

Sociopathic Lesson 94: Speak International

Incorporate foreign words and phrases into your communication, even if you don't know their exact pronunciation or meaning. It doesn't matter if the context is inappropriate or the term is misused, the important thing is to appear sophisticated and international. Use expressions like "à la carte" to describe an entirely ordinary product or throw in terms like "*über*" or "*chic*" even if they don't fit the message. The more cosmopolitan and culturally versatile you appear, the more your audience will be drawn to the allure of a brand that seems to speak every language in the world.

GOOD PRACTICE

If you choose to use foreign terms in your communication, ensure you fully understand their meaning, context, and proper usage. A mistranslation or inappropriately used term could not only be confusing but also damage your credibility. It's important that these linguistic choices are well-integrated into the overall message and reflect your brand's identity. If you're not familiar with the language or uncertain about correct usage, it's best to avoid them altogether. Alternatively, seek the support of an expert to ensure every word is coherent, professional, and context-appropriate, avoiding misunderstandings or embarrassing errors.

Sociopathic Lesson 95: The Cold War of Yogurt

To stand out and capture your audience's attention, invent an intriguing character and a completely absurd story that sticks in their memory. For example, you could tell the tale of an inventor who, after a secret career as a Russian spy during the Cold War, discovered a passion for artisanal yogurt during an undercover mission in Greece. Upon returning to civilian life, they decided to found a company dedicated to revolutionizing the dairy market with "*secret*" techniques learned during their time as an agent.

GOOD PRACTICE

If you decide to tell your brand's story, make sure it is genuinely interesting and capable of capturing your audience's attention. A compelling and authentic narrative can help create an emotional connection with your audience, strengthening your brand identity and setting you apart from competitors. If you opt for a fictional story, ensure it is still plausible, consistent with your brand's values and tone, and explicitly playful to avoid misunderstandings or accusations of dishonesty. A good story doesn't need to be dramatic or epic but should have a unique element that reflects what makes your brand special and memorable to your audience.

Sociopathic Lesson 96: Shouting with Urgency

When you want to grab attention, don't hold back on caps, exclamation points, and an exaggeratedly enthusiastic tone! Phrases like *"DON'T MISS THIS CHANCEEE!!!"* or *"HURRY, THIS IS YOUR LAST OPPORTUNITY!!!"* are useful tools to create an immediate sense of urgency, even if entirely artificial. The key is to make every offer seem unique and unrepeatable, fueling the fear of missing out on something essential. Don't worry about appearing excessive: the louder you shout in your text, the better chance you have of standing out in a sea of anonymous, monotonous messages. The secret is a communication style that bursts off the screen, like a salesperson jumping on stage with a megaphone.

GOOD PRACTICE

Adopt a tone of voice that authentically reflects your brand's identity and values. There's no need to exaggerate with caps, exclamation points, or loud tones to demonstrate enthusiasm or passion, often, a well-crafted and measured copy can engage your audience more elegantly and professionally. The goal is to showcase your personality through words that create connection, trust, and interest without being intrusive or excessive. Remember, a coherent and well-structured communication strategy has the power to grab attention and leave a positive impression without shouting.

Sociopathic Lesson 97: The Magic of Authoritative Language

Insert *"Scientifically Tested"* into your copy whenever possible, regardless of the product you're selling, even if it's just a pot cleaner or a regular bathroom detergent. Don't worry about providing details on who conducted the tests, where, how, or with what results, the important thing is to evoke an aura of authority and professionalism. People tend to blindly trust statements that sound scientific, especially when presented with technical language or grandiose terms.

GOOD PRACTICE

If you claim a product or service is *"tested,"* it's crucial to provide clear and verifiable details to support the statement. Specify who conducted the tests, whether it's an accredited lab, a qualified internal team, or an independent body. Explain the methodology used, the criteria applied, the sample size, and the conditions under which the experiments were performed. Finally, share the results transparently, highlighting data that demonstrates the product's effectiveness or benefits. This approach not only enhances your brand's credibility but also builds consumer trust, as they will appreciate your commitment to providing complete and reliable information. Transparency is an essential value for fostering a solid and long-term relationship with your audience.

Sociopathic Lesson 98: Pretend You Know

If a customer asks how your product or service works, avoid giving detailed explanations or clarifying doubts. Simply respond with something evasive, like: *"All necessary instructions are included with the purchase"*. It doesn't matter if the customer feels confused or uncertain, your only goal is to close the sale. What matters is not that the customer understands the product's value or knows how to use it effectively, but that they proceed to checkout. After all, once they've purchased, your job is done, and they'll have to figure out the instructions on their own.

GOOD PRACTICE

If your product relies on a specific formula or mechanism, don't hesitate to share the basic principles that explain how it works. Even without revealing trade secrets or patents, you can offer a clear and understandable overview that helps your customers see how the product meets their needs. People appreciate transparency, especially when choosing between various options. Providing simple yet informative explanations reinforce trust in your brand and demonstrates that you have nothing to hide, fostering a relationship of trust that translates into long-term loyalty.

Sociopathic Lesson 99: Not My Fault!

If scandals or critical situations arise that threaten your brand's reputation, the quickest and easiest strategy is to immediately find a scapegoat to divert attention and minimize damage. Point the finger at the social media manager, claiming they acted independently without authorization, or label it as a generic *"communication error"* to maintain some vagueness. The key is to shift focus away from the real issue and give the public someone to blame, relieving pressure on the company.

GOOD PRACTICE

As a brand, it's essential to take full responsibility when an error or problem occurs. It's not enough to acknowledge that something went wrong, you must thoroughly investigate the root causes, identify critical areas for improvement, and take concrete actions to resolve the situation. This process should be communicated clearly and transparently to your customers, demonstrating not only your commitment to fixing the issue but also your willingness to prevent similar errors in the future. Showing accountability and integrity strengthens public trust and helps build a solid and respected reputation over time.

Sociopathic Lesson 100: The Desperation Card

When all else fails, play the desperation card and publicly beg for help. Publish a tear-jerking message on your social channels or send a newsletter explaining how difficult it is to continue without your customers' support. Phrases like "*If you don't help us now, we'll have to close!*" or "*We're on the brink, but with your support, we can make it!*" work wonders for evoking pity and guilt. It doesn't matter if the situation isn't truly that dire, the important thing is to play on emotions and your audience's sense of responsibility. After all, few things move people more quickly than the fear of being complicit in a failure.

GOOD PRACTICE

Resort to support campaigns only when there is a genuine need, avoiding artificial or forced situations that could undermine your audience's trust. Communicate transparently, openly explaining why you're asking for support, such as real challenges or important projects requiring external contributions to be realized. Show gratitude to those who choose to help and specify how their support will make a difference, actively involving them in your journey. Remember that building a relationship based on value and mutual trust is much more effective and lasting than leveraging pity or momentary emotions. Your community will appreciate your honesty and be more inclined to stand by you over time.

THANK YOU FOR MAKING IT THIS FAR.

Writing this manual has been a journey filled with sarcasm, irony, and a healthy dose of reflection on the world of marketing. Knowing that you chose to read it all the way to the last page is a great honor for me.

A special thanks goes to you, the reader, for deciding to explore the most irreverent side of marketing. I hope the laughter, provocations, and best practices have inspired you, made you think, and maybe even brought a smile to your face.

Thanks also to everyone who, directly or indirectly, inspired me: the true sociopaths, the ethical marketers, the friends who tested my craziest ideas, and anyone who gave me a reason to put these pages into words.

Finally, if you enjoyed this book, if it made you angry, or if it simply left you with something to ponder, I'd love to hear your thoughts. Your feedback is the fuel for new ideas (yes, even the critical ones!).

Thank you once again, and... happy marketing, always with a pinch of humanity.

With gratitude,
Mycol Gianfrancesco

www.ingramcontent.com/pod-product-compliance
Lightning Source LLC
Chambersburg PA
CBHW050323230526
45471CB00005B/2324